La Vida Es Un Sueno

Minnie Lizette Rivas

authorHOUSE®

AuthorHouse™
1663 Liberty Drive
Bloomington, IN 47403
www.authorhouse.com
Phone: 1 (800) 839-8640

Published by AuthorHouse 10/23/2015

ISBN: 978-1-5049-3411-4 (sc)
ISBN: 978-1-5049-4768-8 (e)

Print information available on the last page.

Any people depicted in stock imagery provided by Thinkstock are models, and such images are being used for illustrative purposes only. Certain stock imagery © Thinkstock.

This book is printed on acid-free paper.

Because of the dynamic nature of the Internet, any web addresses or links contained in this book may have changed since publication and may no longer be valid. The views expressed in this work are solely those of the author and do not necessarily reflect the views of the publisher, and the publisher hereby disclaims any responsibility for them.

Preface

When I first started doing research on dads poems I just wanted to get dads poems together On paper. I wanted to leave my three sons Edward, Mario Adam, Moroni and my future generations, the poems, the reason I say poems is because It is easier to say it, even though it might be prose or short stories, everybody calls them poems, after I got them together. I translated them then I decided to write a few Things about each poem, A song for each one too finally to write mom and dads story, "La vida es un Sueno" It has taken so many years to write it. Many times I have stopped and decided to just forget about it. But my sister Esther has been very instrumental in making me continue mom and dads story and to translate everything, first dads poems from Spanish to English and then my songs and poems from English to Spanish. She would tell me off and I would tell her that for sure I will start on the story soon. She would tell me that she could get some one else in the family to finish the story but I told her they have to go through the headaches I have gone through. One day I decided that I needed to finish what I had started. I was at the very end of the story and the thought that I was almost finishing my project made me very eager to work harder.

Ballad of Telesforo

I want to tell a ballad of a man which has
Already died but his beloved memory is
Still with me today, Telesforo Rivas was his
Name and a mystery he took to the grave.
No one really knows if he did away with his
Sorrows? The man was a poet and also a
Fisherman, he was at his job before the sun
Came out. he was well known throughout
The Texas Gulf Coast. Many people admired
Him and some truly loved him. He spend half
A century speaking of his love, every thing
Which is precious he spoke of this in rythm,
Yes he spoke of the flowers, love should never
Be left out, I will not kneel to the gold it is not
My God. It was after twelve in the afternoon
When the news came of his death. His
Family and friends received it real sad, we will
Never again hear such a manly and tender voice.

Madrigal for Telesforo Rivas

From the waves, down the shell roads of Palacios, I heard them go,
The Night Winds went stalking, throughout the town they blow,
November Winds bending everything with the cold, what say this night?
Have you seen the old poet Telesforo, in shadows or by moonlight?
"We saw him walking down the pier to the tavern by the bay,
   He spoke to us with words of rhyme until he went his way,
   Down to the Sea went Telesforo, to the grey waves and shores,
   The Dark Sea, then may know why the old man is seen no more"

The soaring gulls cry, the sea roars and the wild waves crash
From the wood docks to the wide Gulf the shrimp boats ever pass.
What of the Fisherman? Thundering See, what secrets do you know?
Has he joined the bones beneath your waves, did there go Telesforo?
"Though I sang of pearls and sunken ships of swift riches to claim
   He never left his free and simple life, and never to me came."
Telésforo! Telésforo! The Sea roars and sounds its thunder
But you came not to the Siren Sea, nor do you lie there under.

Through the grasslands the rolling River runs from spring to fall
I asked of Telésforo Rivas and it sang a mournful madrigal.
"In a lonely room I heard his cry. There bitter grapes he sought
   His poetry and countless memories are all that He has got
   His daughters, son and wife so sad they laid him to his rest.
   And for awhile in sleep he lies, bourne upon earth's breast"
   Telésforo, poet of river and sea shall ever by them remain,
   his harp is where the olive tree grows, until tis by him reclaimed.

Chapter 1

Our Ancestors

I was very eager to finish Mom-Dad's story but I decided to write something about our ancestors, they came to America from Spain, after Columbus discovered America in 1492, We don't know when the king of Spain gave them portions of land here in America and Mexico but our ancestors lost all they had in America because of the Guadalupe Hidalgo Rio Grand, Treaty they lost their land but they didn't lose the mineral rights to their portions of land. Telesforo Rivas Sr and his wife Josephine lived in Refugio, Texas in 1800s later on his son Prudencio Rivas moved with all his family to Palacios Texas. We found this account in the 1850 cencis. I believe that someone told Prudencio that there was a lot of work in the fishing industry, In Palacios, Texas, My mothers father and brothers worked in the fishing industry also. Mom said that they went shopping in the fishing boats.

There is another account in the history books in Spain that talk about a voyage taken by Rivas and Iuirarte, to the new territory called North America, this group landed in Matagorda, county and while they were scouting around the area they found the ship that La Salle and his company came in to their surprise, the ship was half way in the water and they never found any of the crew or Lasalle himself. After a while I don't know how long they went back to Spain and reported the tragic news to France, we found this in a magazine in Matagorda, county, this is all that I could find to my surprise I found out that the last name Rivas Iuirarte is one of my sons name but through the years the name became Quirarte instead of Iuirarte someone made a mistake in the spelling, I don't know where the mistake was made but I know that there are Many people that have the last name Rivas here in the United States, Central America South America, and Mexico.

Chapter 2

<hr>

The Dream

I had a dream between 1992 and 1994, This happened about ten years after I had been working on Mom And dads story, The dream I dram, I didn't understand. In the dream I was at mom's house. She told me to go to a big old fashioned purse and get something out. When I got close to the Purse, I noticed that there were millions of little bugs on it they were every where Outside and inside, I told mom in a shocking voice, "The purse is covered with bugs," To which she said very calmly, "Don't be afraid they won't harm you," I did as she said, and to my surprize the bugs didn't bother me in any way, I got a gold coin out, I looked at it and told mom in a shocking voice mom, the coin has my picture on it, to which she replied again "I know," When I woke up the next day, I thought about the dream that I dram during the night, but I didn't know what it meant? It wasn't very long after I had the dream that mom called me to ask me if I could help her look for some life insurance papers which were in some boxes and also in an old trunk from World War II, it belonged to one of my uncles that went to fight in the United States and Korean war, I decided to go visit mom one day after I got off work. Mom seemed happy to see me, and I was very happy to see her. She asked me how my three sons were doing? And I assured her that they were all fine. I started looking for the Life Insurance papers right away, I had been looking for five or ten minutes. When I found the insurance papers, after that I spotted some of dad's old letters, old bills, pictures and poems, I showed mom what I had found "And told her,

3

"That I could use some of the material That I had found," she said,"Take whatever you need and good luck." I also asked mom when and how she thinks that dad made some of the poems, She gave me an inside to some of the poems, She said, That dad made the poem,

The Rose,

For his mother Rosa" I remembered that when grandmother Rosa was alive she would tell us, "Hurry, and get the water hose the plants are dying, And these clouds don't want to give a drop of dew." The poem about the baby bird, mom couldn't remember but she said that, "probably your dad found a baby bird that had fallen from his nest to the ground and his dad Prudencio didn't waste time to tell your dad that the baby bird should have waited for his father to bring him something to eat instead of trying to fly." After mom left the room, I Just stood holding the notebook in my hands, thinking about the things that mom had told me, I also thought about the early days of my childhood some days were good but some were very painful.

Minnie Lizette Rivas

One Bright and Sunny Day

One bright and sunny day, when the
Afternoon aspired, a cloud passed rapidly
In a rapid run, as it passed it saw a flower
That was
Trying to hold on to dear life but it was
   dying in painful agony,
   "Have Pity, Have pity,
Give me a drop of dew,"
The proud cloud says to the dying flower
   As It passes by without any care, "I cannot
Serve such a noble rose," The proud cloud
Returns later in the day, "Wake up, Wake up,
   It is me, I bring you happiness,"
But the rose could not respond
   It had withered and died.

the rose,

when you journey to Sevilla don't forget to stop to see my garden of flowers, they are very lovely indeed
and if you are not in a hurry I want for you to come and see my rose, she is the owner of my soul, she said
that she would very soon return to me and that she loved me so. And if you see her tell her that I'm
lonely and as the days pass my nights are so restless and it seems like I see her face in my dreams.

Minnie Lizette Rivas

In A Shady Jungle Parasol

In a shady Jungle parasol a bird in a nest I saw
   from that nest a baby bird chirps and cries
   his good father has heard him, I am going
   to get good grains for you, Please do not move
   and try to be wise. As the Father slowly left
The nest the baby bird Enviably thought,
   "Oh how I wish that I could fly," As he extended
   his little wings in his intent to fly, a terrible death
   was met by the disobedient son.

Chapter 3

The Early Years

It was very early in the morning when dad would get up to go to work, he tried not to make noise for my mom and nine children. I could hear him in the kitchen and could smell the coffee brewing in an old fashioned coffee maker. He would eat some sweet bread, with coffee, or bacon and eggs if he had time. After he had eaten, he hurried to the boat docks. They were about three blocks from our old house. He was a fisherman by profession. He would go to work on the fishing boats to the Gulf of Mexico. We lived in the small coastal town of Palacios Texas. My mother Apolonia Gatica Rivas was born in Palacios Texas in 1916. My father Telesforo Flores Rivas was also born in Palacios, Texas in 1909. My parents got married in Bay City, Texas in 1935, it was a beautiful day indeed. I found a letter that he wrote to my mom, before they were married. I composed a song using the main thought behind the letter that dad made for my mom.

I will include it in my parents story.

Minnie Lizette Rivas

Keep These Things in Your Mind

Today I come to greet you and to see if
you can begin to think of a sincere
yes or no in your commitment for marriage,
a sincere husband you shall have as a slave
In your every wish keep this things in your mind,
If another person shall come and ask for your
hand in marriage, you are free to marry,
you will never be without love,
"Just remember your parents wish is what you
should persue, "keep these things in your mind,
"If a whirlwind should come? Please don't faint
and in all the discontent which is all around us
give me a sincere yes or no in your commitment
for marriage."

Just Like You

Just like you there will never be another just like you
There will never be some one, which can speak so many
Words of love and passion, your the one for me my love,
The only one. If the night that I saw you the stars were
Shining and my heart inside my chest was beating fast
All at once I knew my life would never be the same when
You said to me "My love you are the one." We had joy for a
Time and for a season, then one day you left me for some
Unknown reason, won't you please come back to me you
Know I love you,? Your the one for me my love the only one.

Chapter 4

Our Mother and Father

My dad was a happy go lucky kind of a guy, my mom was shy and quiet. After living with my dad a few years she started joking and saying funny things. She is a very good, kind hearted, loving person, the kind of friend someone would never want to lose, the same goes for her relatives, they love her very much, these and hundreds more are the reasons why I wrote this poem for mom.

Our Mother

Our mother is like the lilly of the valley,
Pure in heart, very sincere she is the
Prettiest rose she gives freely of her
Sweet smelling perfume to all who pass
Her by, she has many friends by her side,
She loves little animals especially dogs,
And cats and is not happy until all are fed,
As the days passed by she proved to be a
Strong tree reaching to the sky, she hates
 Gossip, she hates a lie, she worked all
 Her life to make us a living, She hardly
Took for herself but did all the giving, may
 God keep our little mother In his loving care,
 We will always be grateful from now until
The very end.

Minnie Lizette Rivas

I Will Wait

My love I shall be waiting until you return,
It really doesn't matter how long I have to Wait,
    I know you really love me, I see it in your eyes
And when I go to sleep at night I see you
    In my dreams, come tell me that you love me,
The way that I love you, and tell me that you
    Will wait forever and a day, If someday
you should leave me, I don't know what I'll do?
I will go somewhere far away, and there I will
    Shurly die, I'm hoping that the morning
    will bring me happiness, and that you will love me
    the way that I love you, It's really sad to dream,
    It's really sad to dream, when there is no hope,
    it's really sad to dream.

Dad working as a fisherman

The life of a fisherman and his family is very difficult, sometimes My dad would make money to support his family, and other times he wouldn't because of bad weather conditions, or if they had problems with the boat, when he couldn't fish he would do boat work or other odd jobs to support the family. Most of the time his co-workers and he would come to land with a good catch of fish and shrimp. They would go to land very happy and celebrate, there was a tavern Close by the bay where they met, dads friends and relatives would crowd around him, because they knew that he could entertain them. Dad would start joking, singing, and saying his poems, After a few beers the other men that were there at the tavern started singing, joking, and saying all kinds of stories, they were a sight to see, this went on until they closed the tavern. By this time the men were tired and hungry, so they went home. Mom was very upset and I'm sure the the other wives were too, but there was nothing they could do about it, that was the life of a fisherman dad would tell mom that they were looking for workers. That someone owed him money and he had to wait for them to pay him. Dad would also tell mom that he started talking to a friend and just couldn't leave him there by himself, and say, "my wife is waiting for me." Most of the time he was telling the truth, mom made him understand that she was not going to put up with his behavior for too long, at first she tolerated him but as time passed, things got worse. When they had problems between them, Mom and the small children would go to my grandmother and grandfathers Simona and Marco Gatica's home, We lived about five blocks from their home. Sometimes it was very cold in winter, or very hot in summer But we had to leave no matter what? We would stay overnight and go home the next day, Dad acted like nothing had happened the night before. My older sisters would tell him what had happened the night before. He always would say he was sorry, but we knew that he could not say no to his friends when it came time to celebrate some kind of event, We knew that the only way things would change, is if he left town, which he did do after a good while. I was very young during this time and didn't know too much about what was going on between mom and dad, One day will forever stay in my mind, It was a beautiful day in summer When dad came home, He wasn't drinking and he was joking and saying funny things, My two brothers and five sisters and I went to greet him outside. Mom was inside cooking and two older sisters were with her helping her get lunch ready, Dad had come home to eat lunch, Dad said that he was mending some nets for a shrimp boat, When he was leaving we all waved goodbye to him, There are a lot of duties to perform before they go out in the water to catch shrimp and fish. In those days you had to buy food and ice To keep The shrimp and fish fresh for about twenty days. Right now there are freezer boats and you can stay as long as you want usually they catch enough in a month or two. This day when dad left to go to work, I kept looking at him walking through a short cut in the back of our house I remember how happy we were all our family was at home. In the evenings we would go to our aunts house a few blocks from our house, We played until late into the night with our cousins. After a while my two sisters and my older brother got married. But I remembered one of those days as so perfect to me even though things weren't perfect to me they were, Anyway I started crying when I remembered some of those perfect days, When I was young, the city of Palacios closed the short cut to the bay after Hurricane Carla stormed into Palacios In 1961, The hurricane took our home and my brothers home which he had build in the back of mom and dads property. After a while Mom and Dad build another home, And my brother build another one too in the back of our home. Moms employers Josephine and her husband Jumpie Plancincio gave a good report about mom and Dad and the city build us another home.

Daniel Rivas his boat in Palacios, TX.

Chapter 5

Strict Environment

My parents were both born in a very strict environment. My mother would tell us how her mother would put all her family to pray every night, there were eleven sisters, and brothers, after she prayed with them she would put them to sleep. After they went to sleep, her mother would pray for about an hour. My fathers mother Rosa Flores Rivas and my grandfather Prudencio Rivas, would make my father go to church when he was young. They were members of the local Spanish Presbyterian Church. As my father grew older, he became more active in church callings. He would give short sermons, and his testimony of God and Jesus Christ at some of the church services. This is where he got his experience in saying his poems in public. When mom and dad got married, they would go to church together. After two years of married life, my sisters, and brothers, and I were born. They had nine children. These are the names of my Sisters and brothers, Betty, Alice, Daniel, Esther, Janie, Myself, Emma, they had one set of twins, Adam and Eve. After we were born and could walk and talk, my grand mother Rosa would also make us go to church, we would make excuses not to go sometimes, but she didn't give up easy and would make us go. I'm so happy that my grandparents were religious, because when we grew older, all of our family became devout members of one church or another. Mom and dad and their children liked several hymns from the Presbyterian church in Spanish, there were two that we liked the most "El Mundo No Puede Ser Mi Hogar," "En La Cruz, En La Cruz, All the members of our family remember these hymns, they bring back memories from our child hood.

Minnie Lizette Rivas

This World is not My Home

I leave the broad road, oh my God,
I want to walk the narrow one, the
World can never understand,
I go to my celestial home.

The world can never be my home,
In heaven is where my mansion is,
The world can never be my home.

Some people want to see me go,
With them through the more wicked lane
I cannot hear them when they call,
I go to my celestial home.

The world can never be my home,
In heaven is where my mansion is,
The world can never be my home.

Oh follow me and sin no more,
Follow the steps of the Savior,
Why don't you look for celestial lands
On high.
The world can never my home,
In heaven is where my mansion is,
The world can never be my home.

My father wrote this poem about Mary and Jesus Christ. He had Studied
the bible and had much respect for Mary and her Beloved Son Jesus

The Woman Mary

Never before the gold or the power
Of the world, shall I kneel,
It doesn't matter if I am oppressed and
Labeled as a tyrant, I may be hungry
   but never humiliated, I may be unjustly
condemned, but I shall never
   be a coward, If sometime an infidel
   shall condemn The man, The woman Mary
   Shall redeem him, blessed be with The
Woman, the man, without her what
Would humanity do? O yes, we are
All free because of Jesus and Mary,
They are Alpha and Omega,
The beginning and the end, We exist
Because of them night and day,
They are a candle that shines,
A brightness that glows.

Minnie Lizette Rivas

Dad showing good morals

My father liked everyone, he didn't care where they lived or how they dressed. Sometimes his friends came to him when they had a problem. He would give them a beer, tell them a poem or Say a joke or two and they would forget their problems for while. He would tell them the poem. "El Diamiante," and "El Dia Fanazul Del Cielo," He tried to show his children good morals Also, when he would tell us these two poems. Spanish Translation is found in the back of the book.

The Diamond

Can a drop of water on a diamond
Fall and because of the mist one
Cannot see so clearly.
? Can a drop of fungus on a diamond
Fall and because of lower it's value
At all? But I tell you, It will never
Lose it's
It's value and it will always be a
Diamond even though the sea my
Spot it.

Water

When I was young I had water,
When I got older I had water,
When I got older, but my three sons
Were young we didn't have water,
I went to my neighbors to ask for water,
But they said, "We barely have for
Ourselves, You need to go into the
Towns and ask for water for you and
For your children." I felt like one of the
Five Virgins of the Bible that didn't get
Enough oil in their lamps, Before the
Bridegroom came into the marriage
Feast, I know that I wasn't ready for
This disaster even though I went to church
Every Sunday, "I was young and didn't
Understand everything In the Bible."
It started raining again so I know
That I needed to do something, I went
To my house and got an umbrella and
Got on top of a table, To ask for water
At first the people were negative and
They said, We have been asking for
Water every day, but no one has brought
Us clean water and we do not have boats
Or anything to go and look for water.
All of a sudden! A city worker came
To let us know that they were giving
The community clean water. As I was
Walking to get the water, I couldn't
Help looking at all the cars, Trucks, Trees,
Trash cans, Lawn chairs, Under the dirty
Water there was junk and stench everywhere.

Minnie Rivas   Pola Rivas

Maria Soto Flores   Rosa Flores

Leon Gatica   Antonio Gatica

Minga   Bessie   Simona   Pola

Aunt Bessie Diaz, Pola Rivas, Dominga Solis

3-12-76

Chapter 6

Politics and Patriotism

Dad's friends would come looking for him when there were celebrations of the fourth of July or the Fiestas Patrias. Dad knew about our forefathers and how they got their freedom from England. He also knew about the civil war here in the United States and how the slaves were freed. Many people liked to hear about The Revolution in Mexico, My grandfather was born in Mexico in the 1800's, He also knew about the father of freedom of Mexico. Miguel Hidalgo y Costilla. He also knew about Pancho Villa and Emelliano Zapata The leaders of the Mexican Revolution and so many brave men that deserve an honorable mention. Francisco Madero was the President of Mexico during The Revolution. It was impossible for poor campesions to own land. Dad knew a lot of history of Mexico even though he was born in Palacios, Texas, he got his information from his father, mother and books that he would read, dad wrote two poems about how Mexico got it's Independence from Spain that one is Cuahtemoc, and the other one is about a campaign of two men running for Governor or Senator in Mexico, Mr Don Luis believes, this poem may be fiction? We never asked dad about this poem.

Minnie Lizette Rivas

Cuahtemoc

Cuahtemoc, yes already dead, would leave
A seed whose name was Miguel Hidalgo
Y Costilla, hundreds of years have passed
But this beloved country of mine the tree
sprouted lively, big, immense, one morning
when getting up from his humble bed he felt
a strong sensation in his chest and he
triumphed in the right for liberty, Why?
In my beloved land, liberty does not faint,
even though life may get agitated an
astronomical voice befalls, Oh how they
claimed to do away with liberty,
Many intruders oh how they tried to do away
with it, but how can they clip it if giants
defend it? We that babble the A B C'S
of science Enthusiastically promise to defend
It With a light from the strange torch, A town which cries but finally is
Redeemed from the

dominion of Mother Spain.

Mister Don Luis Caballero Believes

Mr. Don Luis believes that a governing seat
is to prepare the workers and to give
his view to the people and sit as winner.
El Tecolate is almost killing himself to
finish what he has to do, but I Luis can go
further in the last run his fierce workers
and friends go back and forth through out
the state to get the necessary votes and over
power El Tecolate, finally they catch up to him.
Mr Don Luis is a friendly rancher and both
runners with a cigars in hand are both giving it
all that they can give, but mister Don Luis
had it all figured out knowing that he will finish
as the winner putting forth a good, and
rough fight, and El Tecolote will have a rough
time paying back bets.

Minnie Lizette Rivas

Freedom

Freedom is a word that I love to hear
Freedom, Freedom, Freedom, ringing
Loud and clear, It has been here with
us from the very start and it will live forever
In mens tender hearts, God gave us this Country
let us not forget and He gave us Jesus
full of grace, He is our commander our banner he'll raise,
Freedom is a word that I love to hear Freedom, Freedom,
Freedom ringing loud and clear, It has
been here with us from the very start and it will live
forever in mens tender hearts, Our soldiers are fighting
in the day and nightTo retain this freedom with much
strength and might,
We will keep on going with our torch in hand
All the different cultures will protect this land.
Freedom is the word that I love to hear Freedom, Freedom,
Freedom, ringing loud and clear, it has been here with us from the
Very start and it will live forever in men's tender hearts,
Let us shout how grateful we will always be,
For this land of plenty for this land so free,
All across America and across the isles,
Hurrah to the Nations who are our allies,

Freedom is the word that I love to hear
Freedom, Freedom, Freedom, ringing loud and clear,
it has been here with us from the
Very start and it will live forever in men's tender hearts.

Chapter 7

Modern Times

The young Women From Our Town

In the early 1950's there were not too many televisions, only the rich or people with money to spare could buy them or people that had good jobs. When my older sisters got married they could afford a Television. For a long time most people could afford just one. During this time people would visit each other all the time. And converse about everything that was happening in the community. The single women would talk about the single Men in town. The single men would talk about the single girls or Women in town. The married people would talk about their spouses and children. The majority of the people would listen to the radio, every one would gather around the radio to listen to the news, weather, and music. Dad had to know about the weather, because at one time he would go out fishing in the Gulf of Mexico. When they didn't go fishing they would meet at their favorite tavern to drink beer, during the winter the sea was very rough so they would spend a lot of their time talking about their adventures At sea. Some of the men liked to go hunting, and talked about the Havalinas, deer, geese, ducks, and who knows what else? The women worked also they worked packing shrimp, fish, and crab in the local factories in town. There were a few women that felt Liberated and the men talked about the women and I'm sure that the wives knew about them too. Dad made a poem about these women.

Minnie Lizette Rivas

The Young Women from our Town

The young women from our town
Have fame galore, In the tavern they
Meet, but they don't meet to talk about
The fish that got away, instead they talk
About the love that got away, after
They find another one they promise to
Be good and to live the life of a married
woman, But after a month or two when
they find them selves in the boring kitchen,
They say, "this life is too sad"
and they return to the tavern.

All of the Lost Children

All of the lost children are going through
The world they have lost everything and they
Don't have faith, they went looking for things
Of the world and the only thing they found
Was pain and suffering, If you have fallen
If you have hit rock bottom, don't lose your
Pride and don't lose your faith, Christ loves
You and He gave his life for you, Christ is the
Same He works in the vineyard. Christ is com-
Ing soon, He is coming for his people, If you are
Not ready get ready today. The good angels
Are looking out for us, All of them want us to
Choose the right things. Christ doesn't see
Race color or anything He only sees what is
In your heart, give him a minute he gave his
Life for you, If you do this you will never be sorry.

Adam R.

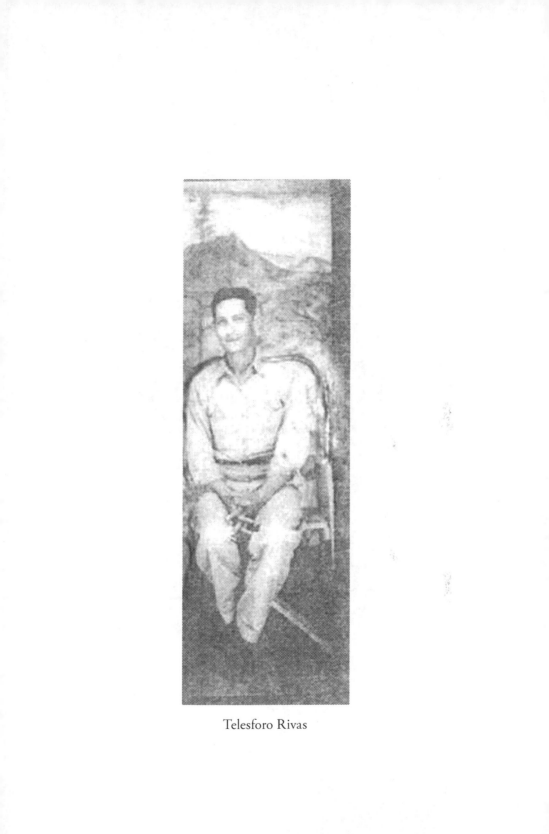

Telesforo Rivas

Minnie Rivas

Top Minnie Rivas

Pola Rivas

Eva R. Minnie R Adam R.

Eva R.   Adam R.

Pola Rivas

Moroni R. Mario Adam R. D.

Bonnie Bu Eddie R. Q

Eddie Q. Moroni, Mario

Minnie, Mario, Moroni

Top Eddie R. Q.   Bottom Right to Left Minnie R. Bobby B. Eddie R. Q

Life Is a Dream

Life is a dream in which we finally
Wake up and find the major small pleasure
The bad is so strong that it crosses
Our path and it runs contrary to the
Light and offering. The joy is born and
die like poppy seeds but the trouble
Lives on always hurting. And when
The tranquility returns with sweet
Illusions the place in the soul is
Occupied by them. It's sad to keep
On walking and living in a world
Which doesn't exist and it's sad to
Keep on living and walking without
Finding any relief, only sadness in
The eyes if there is delirium, there
Is more thisle and thorn. The joy is
Born but die like poppy seeds,
But the trouble lives on, always hurting,
And when the calmness returns with
Sweet illusions the trouble is
Embedded deep in the soul.

Rosa Flores
Carol English
Edwin Young
Bobbie Buckley
Bonnie Buckley

8-5-01
Minnie Rivas
Austin Diaz   Alena Diaz   Adrian Diaz

Eddie, Mario, Minnie Rivas 1979

Maroni, Mario, Minnie Rivas

Kateland Diaz

Chapter 8

What a Precious Love

What a precious love, what a precious heaven,
What a precious moonglow, What a precious sun
I love him very much, Because he feels everything
That I also feel, Please come close to me, I want for
Your hands to hold me in a thousand ways, I want to
Be in your heart, give me more love but more and more
I want for you to kiss me the way you kiss me and then
you leave, I understand that my soul shouldn't love you
so much but I feel yours calling me and I just can't help
myself, What a precious love, What a precious Heaven,
What a precious moonglow, What a precious sun,
If something inside me changed it's because of you
Because of that love that so many wanted you gave
It to me, What a precious love.

Chapter 9

The following poem was written by my dad, When he came back to Palacios after being gone for many years, The title is, "The light of the coin, I'm very happy that he came back so we can understand what he went through, While he was living in Aransas Pass, Texas close to his brother Manuel Rivas, His wife Ramona, And their children. I believe that he wanted for us to know about his life and his experiences, while he had been gone, Dad always hoped that he and mom would get back together again, Because they never divorced, He was always welcome at our home. I wrote two songs about lost love.

The Light of the Coin

At one time I was the love of your life
The only thing that is left is the hurt
I can't understand why you lie?
Why is your love so indifferent and
Our friendship so unimportant?
You see the light of the coin
But you don't see the sad man that has
No one to turn to in his hour of need,
Today only pain exists and no good in
The world can erase it.

Minnie Lizette Rivas

The Light From Heaven

Right here I have a ring, My Lord, MY God
Of diamonds and of Gold, And also other
Treasures which all the world seeks for, but
Even though I have the shiny earthly things,
The thing I most desire, Is the pure light from
Heaven, Today I find myself so lonely and so
Blue, I feel so all alone My God my faith is more
Than due, I am also your daughter which struggles
And she dreams, Today I come to you for help with
This problem so immense, My Jesus is happy when
I choose the right things, I want something much better,
And clearly more profound, I want the love of
Jesus, He really gives you comfort, The thing I most
Desire is the pure light from Heaven

An Extra Coin

As I sit here a thinking with a bottle in my right hand. I think about the past and how it used to be and as the days, the weeks, The months pass, and everything is new, My thoughts are still encircled in the fact that I love you, You left me for another right now I feel real sad, sweetheart I really love you, you really hurt me bad, you changed your way of walking, you changed your way of talking, you changed me for another I don't know if I can go on? I know you love the diamonds, I know you love the gold, you changed me for another I

Don't know if I can go on, I really

Don't know what happened but as I

Sing this song, you left me for another, which had an extra coin.

Chapter 10

Balada de Telesforo

El mar obscure quisas sepan porque el hombre
Anciano no se ha visto ya mas? Las gaviotas volantes
    Lloran, El mar rujie y las olas salvages pegan de los
    mulles al golfo grande, Los barcos de pescar camaron
    Y pescado pasan,? Que pasa con el Pescador?
    Mar que retumbas, Que secretos connoces?
        Halli se fue Telesforo? A pesar que yo le hable de perlas
Y barcos debajo de tus olas que quisas tengan riquesas
Para reclamar, el nunca dejo su vida libre y sin prejuicos
    Y nunca a mi vino. "Telesforo!
"Telesforo! El mar ruje, suena, y retumba
Pero nunca veniste al mar sereno, ni descansas halli
Debajo, por el valle el rio corre de Primavera ha Otonio,
    yo preguente por Telesforo Rivas y canto una triste madrigal.
    "En un cuarto muy triste lo oie llorar, y busco ubas amargas
    Sus poecia y tantas memorias son todo lo que
    le queda. Sus hijos su esposa muy triste lo lleban a su
Descansa, donde el duerme por un tiempo,
Descansa en el pecho de la tierra, Telesforo, Telesforo, poeta
Del rio y el mar seguiera con su harpa arriba donde se encuentra
    El arbol de los olivos, hasta que de nuevo todo sea por el
Reclamado.

Chapter 11

EL dia Fan Azul Del Cielo

El dia fan azul del cielo, cuando la tarde aspiraba,
Cruzaba en un rapido vuelo una nube pasajera,
Viera al pasar una flor que abrasada se moria
en su penosa agonia, dijole asi con amor,
"por piedad" "por piedad" una gota de rocio.
Dice la nube orgullosa insensible caminando,
"No puedo server a tan noble Rosa"
Vuelve La nube orgullosa, Despierta yo soy despierta,
Yo te traigo La alegria mas la flor no respondia.
La infeliz estaba Muerta.

la Rosa,

cuando viajes a Sevilla no te olvides de visitor mi jardin de flores que son
bonitas de verdad

y si no llevas prisa te invito a ver la rosa mas Hermosa que es la duena de
todo mi ser.

ella dijo que pronto a mi lado regreseria y que ella tambien a mi me queria.

y si la ves dile que me siento triste y asi pasa el tiempo la estrano mas y
mas cada dia

y si la ves dile que la quero mucho y entre suspiros y suenos parece que veo
su linda carita.

En Una Selva Sombria

En una Selva Sombria, un nido en un arbol vi,
Desde aquel nido pia, pia, un pajarillo,
Su buen padre que lo ha oido,
Voy a volar ricos granos a traerte,
Esperame sin moverte y procura ser juicioso,
Al ver el nido dejar, Dijo el candido poyuelo,
"Cuanto embidio y cuanto anhelo" Quiso en el
Acto volar desendio rapidosamente, Y horrible
Muerte encontro, el hijo desobediente.

Chapter 12

Nuestra Madre

Nuestra madre es como el aleli del valle,
Pura de Corazon, Muy sincera, Sin duda
Es es la rosa mas bonita, Ella da de su
Perfume a todos los que pasan por su jardin,
Ella tiene muchas amistades a su lado,
Le gustan los perros y los gatos, Y no esta
Con tenta hasta que todos comen, Asi
Pasaron los dias y ella provo ser como un
Arbol que casi lleega al cielo, No le gusta el
Chisme, Ni la mentira, Ella trabajo toda su
Vida, Ella no penso en si misma, Nada mas
En su familia, Que Dios guarde a nuestra
Madracita en su cuidado amoroso, Estamos
Muy contenta por tenerla aqui en este mundo
Terrenal, Estamos muy agradecidos de hoy
Hasta el final.

Minnie Lizette Rivas

Te Esperarare Mi Amor

Te esperare mi amor hasta que tu regreses no
Importa cuanto tiempo te tenga que esperar,
Yo se que tu me quieres me lo dicen tus ojos
Y tambien en mis suenos halli excistes tu,
Ven dime que me quieres como te quiero yo
Y dime que me esperas por siempre hasta el
Final, Si un dia te alejaras? No se lo que yo
Haria? Me ire lojos de aqui y halli yo moriria
Espero que la manania me traiga la alegria y
Que me quieras tu igual que yo mi vida,
Qui triste es sonar, Que triste es sonar, Cuando
No hay Consuelo, Que triste es sonar
Mi papa trataba de ensenarnos buenas morales con esta poesia

El Diamiante

? Puede una gota de fango en un diamante caer
Y por causa de la neblina no tan claro se pueda ver,?
?Puede una gota de fango en un diamiante
Caer y tambien de ese modo su valor
Desmerecer.? Pero no importa que de fango
Se encuentre lleno no perdera su valor por
Un instante y siempre sera diamiante por mas
Que lo manche el seno.

Minnie Lizette Rivas

Agua

Cuando estaba joven tenia agua,
Cuando estaba un poco mas vieja tenia agua
Cuanto estaba un poco mas vieja pero mis
Hijjos estaban joven no tenia agua, Fui con mis
Vecinos a pedir agua pero ellos me dijeron nada
Mas tenemos para nosotros vaya a las ciudades
A pedir agua "Me senti como una de las cinco
Virgins de la Biblia, Cinco estaban listas y cinco
No estaban listas, Yo iba a la igliesa cada Domingo
Pero yo era joven y no entendia todo lo que esta
En la Biblia. Regrese a mi casa y coji un parabrisas
Me fui a la calle me sube en una messita y empeze
A pedir agua despues de un rato nos avisaron que
Ya estaban dando agua en cierta lugar de distri-
Bucion. me senti muy contenta, empeze a caminar
Rumbo al lugar de distibucion. No pude evitar de ver
Todo lo que estaba a mi alrededor, Coches, arboles,
Sillas de sentarse a fuera. debajo del agua y habia muchos
Escombros por dondequiera, y apestaba mucho.

El Mundo No Es Mi Hogar

La senda ancha dejare yo quiero por la angosta andar
Y muchos no sabran porque, Mas voy a mi Celeste
Hogar1 No puede el mundo ser mi hogar en Gloria tengo
Mi mansion, No puede el mundo ser mi hogar.
Algunos quieren verme ir por el sender de maldad
Oir no puedo su llamar, pues voy a mi Celeste Hogar:
Oh ven conmigo picador, Y sigue en pos del Salvador.
Porque? No quieres tu buscar, La hermosa tierra mas
Alla? No puede el mundo ser mi hogar: En Gloria tengo
Mi masion No puede el mundo ser mi hogar.

Chapter 13

Patrotismo y Politica

Cuactemoc

Cacutemoc ya muerto dejaba una semilla
Que se llamaba Miguel Hidalgo y Costilla
Muchos anos yah an pasado Pero Luego
Patria mia el arbol brotaba altivo, gigante,
Inmenso. Una manana levantose de su
Lecho se produjo una tempestad en su
Pecho Y lanso trunfante el derecho a la
Libertad, Porque! En mi patra bendita
La libertad no desmaya, mas la vida se
Ajita pero con potencia infinita su voz
Austrante estalla. O clamaron apagala
Varios cautiveros, Pero como apagarla
Como clipsarla si la defenden, gigantes,
Nosotros que balbucimos el ABC de la
Sciencia antustias prometemos

Creen Don Luis Caballero

Creen Don Luis Caballero que gobernar un estado
De elementos es prepar ar los asientos para
Sentarse en su lugar, El Tecolote matarse pa
Prepararse en la parte que falta, Pero yo Luis le
Pego salta en la ultima parajura, Su canditatura
Por dificultosa tambien es cara, Sus partideros
Atroces recoren todo el estado de emburo
Enparajado, Para echarse al Tecolote, Don Luis
Es un gran amigote, Que paraja par con puro,
Tiene al Tecolote en un cuero duro, Bien compuesto
Y encerado y le da la emparejada esperando ganar
A lo Rudo.

Minnie Lizette Rivas

Libertad

Libertad es lo que me gusta escuchar
Libertad, Libertad, libertad sonando fuerte
Y claro, Ha estado aqui desde el principio,
Y vivira por siempre en los corazones tiernos
De los hombres,
Dios nos dio este pais y que no olvidemos,
Dios nos mando a Jesus Christro y el deramo su
Sangre, Jesus nunca falto en nada y esta lleno
De gracia, El es nuestro Comandante nuestra
Bandera el alsara, Libertad, Es lo que me gusta
Escuchar, Libertad, libertad, libertad, Sonando
Fuerte y claro, Nuestros soldados estan peliando
De dia y de noche, Para retener esta libertad con
Mucha fuerza y esfuerso, Estaremos luchando
Con la antorcha en la mano, Todas las differentes
Culturas protegeran esta nacion, Libertad es lo
Que me gusta escuchar, Libertad, Libertad, Libertad,
Sonando fuerte y claro, Dejanos gritar lo agrecidos
Que estamos por esta tierra de abundanzia y libre,
Al cruzar America y al cruzar las islas, Ra, Ra, Ra,
A las naciones que estan con nosotros, Libertad es
Lo que me gusta escuchar, Libertad, Libertad,
Libertad, Sonando fuerte y claro, Ha estado aqui
Desde el principo, y vivira siempre en los corazones
Tiernos de los hombres.

Que Bonito Amor

Que bonito amor, que bonito cielo, que bonita luna
Que bonito sol. Dame mas amor pero mas y mas,
Quiero que tus manos me hagan mil caricias, Quiero
Estar en ti, dame mas amor pero mas y mas quiero
Que me beses como tu me besas y despues te vas,
Yo commpro que mi alma en la vida no tiene derecho
A quererte tanto pero siento que tu alma me grita me
Pide carino y nomas no me aguanto,
Que bonito amor, que bonito cielo, que bonita luna
Que Bonito sol, Si algo en mi cambio te lo debo a ti
Porque aquel carino que qusieron tantas me lo
Diste a mi, Que bonito amor.

Chapter 14

Tiempos mas Modernos

Las Muchachas de Mi Pueblo

Las muchachas de mi pueblo tienen fama
Con regor en las tabernas se juntan
Para buscar un nuevo amor, no se juntan
Para hablar del pescado que se les fue,
Sin decir porque hablan del amor que se
Les fue, despues que se encuentran otro
Juran ser bunas y hondras, y hacer vida de
Casadas, pero despues de un meso das que se
Encuentran en la bojornosa cocina Dicen,
"Esta vida es muy triste y se regresen a la
Taberna."

Los Hijos perdidos

Los hijos perdidos vagan por el mundo,
Han perdido todo ya no tienen fe se fueron
En busca de cosas del mundo y solo encontraron
Penas y dolor si tu has cayado hasta el mero fondo
No pierdas tu orgullio no pierdas la fe, Christo a ti
Te ama port ti dio la vida, El sigue lo mismo
Trabaja en la vina. Christo viene pronto viene
Por su gente, si tu no estas listo ponte listo hoy
   Los Angeles Buenos por nosotros velan todos
Ellos queren que escojes el bien Christo no ve raza
Ni color ni nada El solo se fija en el corazon,
Dale un momento Por ti dio la vida y veras que nunca
    te arepentaras, Christo viene pronto viene por su gente,
    Si tu no estas listo pon te listo hoy, Christo a tite ama
    Por ti dio la vida, el sigue el mismo trabaja en la vina.

Chapter 15

La Vida Es Un Sueno

La vida es un sueno del cual al fin encontramos
El major plazer pequeno, tan fuerte los males
Que corren por entre la zenda que corren
En contra la luz y la ofrenda,
Los goces nacen y mueren como puras
Asusanas mas las penas viven siempre
Y siempre yeren y cuando vuelve la calma
Con las illusions bellas, Su lugar dentro
Del alma queda ocupada por ellas.
Que triste es viver sonando en un mundo
Que no existe y que triste es seguir viviendo,
Y caminiando sin ver un alivio solo delerio
En los ojos, que si hay en la vida deliros,
Son mucho mas los abrojos, los goses nacen
y mueren como puras acusanas mas las penas
Viven siempre y siempre yeren,
Y cuando vuelve la calma con las illuisones
Bellas su lugar dentro del alma queda ocupada
por ellas.

Chapter 16

Dad Returns Home

La Luz Del Dinero

En un tiempo fui el amor de tu vida,
Hoy ya no queda nomas la herida,
"?Porque finjes, porque mientes
Porque es tu amor tan ligero?"
Cuan Amistad avacia,
Cuando brilla la luz del dinero,
Y no ves al hombre triste cuando
No tray socorre, Hoy solo el dolor
Existe sin que haya bien que lo borre."

Minnie Lizette Rivas

Aqui tengo un anillo

Aqui tengo un anillio, Senor mi Dios,
Que es de puro oro, Y tambien otras
Prendas que brillan y son bellas,
Pero a pesar de todas las cosas que yo
Tengo, lo que yo mas deseo es pura luz
Del cielo, Senor hoy me encuentro,
Sin vida y sin luz me encuentro sin
Sostento cargando voy mi cruz,
Yo soy tambien tu hija, que lucha y
Que suena hoy viene a que le ayudes
A olvidar inmensa pena, Jesus esta
Contento que escoga yo lo bueno,
Quiero algo mas bonito y tambien mas
Profundo, quiero el amor de Christo
El si que da consulo, Lo que yo mas
Deseo, Es pura luz del Cielo.

Otra Moneda

Mientras me siento aqui con una botella
De vino en mi mano derecha pienso en
El pasado y como todo fue y mientras
Los dias, pasan y tambien los meses, todo es
Nuevo menos yo y mi amor por ti, Me dejaste
Por otro y ahora me siento mal, Mi amor deveras
Te amaba y me lastimaste mucho, Cambiaste
Tu modo de caminar, Cambiaste tu modo de hablar,
Me cambiaste por otro no se si pueda seguir,
Te gustan los diamiantes, Te gusta tambien el oro,
Me dejaste por otro no se si pueda seguir,
Sen realidad no se lo que paso?
Pero mientras canto esta cancion, Me dejaste por
Otro que tenia otro moneda.

Minnie Lizette Rivas

Ahora Si Ya Se Por Cierto

Ahora si ya se por cierto y si muero yo por dentro
Es que tu amor perdi, No fue facil el perderte,
Prefierible fue la muerte, Que olvidarme, Yo de ti,
No pensaste que alguin dia, De todo me cansaria
No pensaste un momento mi amor, es por eso
Que no queda ni tan solo una esperanza, Siento
Que te he perdido por tan larga la distancia.
Tu fallaste tu bien sabes y volaste como una ave
Pa otros rumbos y otros amores, Ahora ya vienes
De Nuevo preguntando, "Si te quiero?" Para que
Andar con quentos se que tu amor perdi.
Por favor ya no me llames, Me molestes, ni implores
Ya es tarde tu bien sabes hasta secas estan las flores.
Tu fallaste tu bien sabes y volaste como una ave pa
Otros rumbos y otros amores, Ajhora ya vienes de nuevo
Preguntando sit e quiero, Para que andar con cuentos
Se que tu amor perdi.
Please add:

Chapter 17

Translation In Spanish

"La Vida Es Un Sueno"

corridor de telesforo rivas
Quiero cantar un corridor de un hombre que ya
Murio pero su recuerdo querido presente lo tengo yo
Telesforo Rivas se llamabay un recuerdo con el se llevo
Nunca en verdad se supo si su pena el sano, era poeta
el hombre tambien era pescador estaba en su trabajo
antes que saliera el sol. el era muy conocido por toda la
costa de de tejas, mucha gente lo admiraba, por todo lo
que les dava, el paso cincuenta anos hablando de su
dolor todo lo que es precioso de esto el declamo. si
declamo de las flores, amor no ha de faltar, al oro no me
arrodio,el oro no es mi altar. ya era de medio dia cuando
la noticia llego, hoy murio nuestro amigo que dios lo tenga
en paz. su hijo ysu esposa, muy triste la recibio, no
volveremos a oir tan varonil y tan dulce voz.

madrigal para telesforo

desde las olas y mas halla de los caminos de palacios
texas los oie ir, los vientos de la noche se fueron
silenciosos por todo el pueblo soplan, vientos de
noviembre doblando todo con el frio,
?que dicen esta noche,? han visto al Viejo poeta
telesforo, en las sombras oh por la luz de la luna?
lo vimos caminando por el mulle para la tavern cerca
de la Bahia, nos hablo con palabras de verso
hasta que se fue por su camino. para el mar
se fue telesforo, para las olas grieces, y la playa,
---------- y el mar obscure quisas sepan porque el hombre
ancinano no se ha visto mas? las gaviotas volantes
lloran, el mar rujie y las olas salvajes pegan de los
mulles al golfo grande, los barcos de pescar camaron
y pescado pasan,?que pasa con el pescador?
mar que retumbas,? que secretos coneces?
halli se fue telesforo? a pesar que yo le hable de perlas
y barcos debajo de tus olas que quisas tengan requesas
para reclamar, el nunca dejo su vida libre y sin prejuicos
y nunca a mi vino, '' telesforo!
"telesforo! el mar ruje, suena, y retumba
pero nunca veniste al mar sereno, ni descansas halli
debajo, por el valle el rio corre de primavera a otono,
yo pregunte por telesforo rivas y canto una triste madrigal,
"en un cuarto muy triste lo oie llorar, y busco ubas amargos
sus poecia y tantas memorias son todo lo que le queda
sus hijos su esposa son todo lo que le queda. sus hijos
su esposa muy triste lo lleban a su descanso, donde el
duerme por un tiempo, descansa en el pecho de la tierra,
telesforo, telesforo poeta del rio y el mar seguiera con su
arpa arriba donde se encuentra el arbol de los olivos,
hasta que de Nuevo todo sea por el reclamado.

Printed in the United States
By Bookmasters